One day in the year 25X when vegetables roamed the earth. There was one potato named Pat. Pat was scrolling on his phone looking for a way to make some extra money. It was while scrolling that he located a rare, rumored ruby. No one has actually ever seen this ruby but in further research he located there was supposedly a map that would lead him to the said ruby. Pat was both nervous about needing to make some money to help with bills but also excited about this idea of a rare, rumored ruby.

As a means to help himself try to relax Pat decided to go on a hike outside of town. As Pat drove to the park for his hike his mind swirled with ideas of what might happen if he were to actually find this ruby? He might get rich or maybe famous, but then again what if there actually is no ruby and it is all just a rumor. Nonetheless Pat decided the best next step was to go for a hike to relax. Pat arrived at the park for his hike and picked a trail he had never hiked before. Pat put on his sunscreen of butter with his cheese slice hat and started out on his hike.

Pat hiked a ways on the trail when located a field of spices. The aroma coming from this field of spices was invigorating and delicious all at the same time. Pat decided to stop for a minute and rest.

While he was sitting in the field he saw some other hikers and they all started talking. Pat introduced himself to Carl the carrot and Chip also a potato. Pat, Carl and Chip were talking about trails they hiked previously, the amazing smell of this spice field, and more. Pat was nervous to share about the rare, rumored ruby. What if they thought it was silly? What if they too were looking for the ruby? Pat opted to keep the conversation to hiking and wild spices.

Carl brought up how he hiked the tallest mountain of salt the previous year. The saltiest mountain had been rough with Carl facing salt storms where he couldn't see where he was hiking half of the time and the rough, hardened terrain where he almost fell and broke his top. Carl stated that he had thought the salt mountain would take about a week to hike up and back down to base; however it ended up taking him almost three weeks.

Carl shared that he had to ration his food, boil stream water to drink and crush rock salt to keep warm. As Carl made it to the top of the tallest salt mountain he looked around and enjoyed the white to gray covered mountain with salt rock formations like he had never witnessed before. Finally back at base he felt proud for staying strong and pushing forward. Pat and Chip applauded Carl for his heroing story and were in awe of his accomplishment.

Chip shared a tale of his recent hillside climb on Cream Hill. Chip reported that he was having a nice, relaxing hike when he at one point encountered a ferocious ant. This ant appeared crazy hungry and Chip feared the ant would eat him in one bite. Chip has studied martial arts for several years but were his martial arts skills enough to overcome this massive, ferocious and hungry ant? Chip was frozen not knowing how to proceed next while the ant stared him down with his teeth grinding.

Chip then realized it wasn't he that the ant was staring at but instead a field of chocolate cupcakes. Chip and the ant both then ran towards the cupcakes and devoured half of the cupcake field until they passed out from overeating.

Pat was still too nervous to share about the ruby so he instead told Carl and Chip that he was new to hiking and that this was actually his first ever hike. Pat inquired with these more advanced hikers, Carl and Chip, as to where might be their favorite or most dreamed about location to hike. Carl and Chip looked at each other simultaneously and then shouted "THE RUBY!!!".

Pat, now conflicted, asked what they were talking about with this ruby. What is the ruby thing they seem so excited about? Carl and Chip are both SOOOOO excited about this ruby that they are talking so very fast, talking over one another, and Pat had no idea what was happening. Finally Carl and Chip stop talking long enough for Pat to ask them to please start over, one at a time and sllooowly share their ruby stories.

Carl went first and shared that he heard the ruby was a powerful gem that would grant him any power that he wanted and even would have the ability to change up his powers as many times as he desired. Chip said that the ruby was the most precious gem ever and worth more money than he could ever need or even want.

Pat was intrigued. The idea that both Carl and Chip knew of the ruby was in itself exciting. The stories that Carl and Chip shared about the ruby made his desire to locate the ruby that much greater. It didn't matter at this point which story about the ruby was correct or maybe even still if it was all just a rumor. Pat though was happy knowing that his two new friends who he just happened to meet today on his hike were dreaming of the same thing as him, and that is to find the truth about the ruby.

Pat asked Carl and Chip if they had ever searched for the ruby. Both said they had only ever dreamt about looking for the ruby. The three of them sat in the spice field now daydreaming about the ruby. They were all so excited! Pat, Carl and Chip all just knew the ruby was more than just a rumor, myth, and dream, but instead believed in all the ruby had to offer each of them.

The three were determined to find the ruby and agreed to team up to see if there really is a rare ruby that will bring them powers and money. As Pat, Carl and Chip daydreamed about all the adventures that they could potentially have with trying to find the ruby the day began to quickly pass and the sun began to set in the spice field. As they were laying there all of the sudden the sun hit a ray of red coming from the left of where they were lying. All three jumped up, grabbed their gear, and ran to see what the red ray was exactly and where it was actually coming from.

Pat, Carl and Chip ran through the spice field past the cinnamon, past the peppercorn, and hurdled over the bacon pan all while the red ray grew in intensity. Soon they arrived at a cave that is bright and sparkling almost as much as their eyes of excitement. Pat, Carl and Chip enter the cave to find statues of the ruby rings. The rings per the legendary stories are the guardians of the ruby. The three are roaming about the cave looking for clues regarding this ruby when they hear a crackling. They turn to see a towering tree of broccoli who is the ring's guardian of the gateway, and he is about to pounce on Pat. Chip though rams the stock of the broccoli guardian and covers him in hot melted cheese that just happened to be in his drink pouch. The broccoli crumbles to bits now lying in florets mixed with melted cheese on the cave's floor. They grab the broccoli guardians key to open the door at the back of the cave.

Once the door is open they feel an immediate heat overpower them, and find red hot cherry tomatoes. The hot cherry tomatoes are hanging high on vines and are giving off a temperature of over 100 degrees. Pat, Carl and Chip are all worried not only about dehydration but also how to get past the hot cherry tomatoes. Carl notices that the tomatoes are sleeping so they tiptoe down the stairwell maze to the base of the steps.

Once at the bottom they find a well of water. Ready to cool off they all drink from the well and take a break. Pat notices while he is getting another drink that there is a key hanging in the well. Carl helps Pat tie a loop on his spork so they can lower it down the well to grab this new key. The well is deep and they are struggling to grab the key when the trio is approached by Queen Tina, the leader of the hot cherry tomatoes.

Pat, Carl and Chip get frightened but their fear quickly fades as Tina is in awe of the trio getting past all her guards so she offers as a reward to help them grab the key in the well. Pat, Carl and Chip are grateful for Tina's help and accept her accolades. With the key in hand Tina guides them all down a secret passage with a door at the end of the hall. While they are walking Pat asks Tina if she has heard the story of the ruby. Tina advised that the ruby has watched over her homeland for a long time and that its light is magnificent.

Together Pat, Carl, Chip and Tina walk towards her homeland. While on their path to Tina's they encounter a monster like no one has seen before. It has the stalk of a broccoli, the body shape of a potato, the coloring of a cherry tomato and the top of a carrot. This rare vegetable combination stands tall against them and begins to throw pepper at them. Tina uses her shield and calls for her soldiers to guard Pat, Carl and Chip.

Under the guidance of Tina and her soldiers they find their way to safety and to Tina's palace. Pat, Carl and Chip are exhausted from their journey today so Tina invites them to dinner and to stay for the night to rest. They are grateful for all Tina has done for them and agree to her hospitality. Pat, Carl and Chip freshen up before dinner and enjoy an amazing royal feast of salads, fruits, and burgers.

After dinner Tina suggests that they can return to their rooms to relax or they are welcome to explore the grounds of the palace. Always the adventurers they opt to roam the palace grounds. In the moonlight they spy a flower garden with a gate that sparkles as bright as the moon and stars.

Pat, Carl and Chip open the gate to find a layer of brightness and happiness that fills the air. Pat, Carl and Chip have located the rare, rumored ruby on the palace grounds. The trio feel as if they might be dreaming but alas they have located the ruby and can now sleep feeling accomplished and proud of all that the day has given them.

The end…or at least until Pat and friends' next adventure.

www.ingramcontent.com/pod-product-compliance
Lightning Source LLC
Chambersburg PA
CBHW042019110726
48006CB00004B/1153